Shira and the Trees

A TU BISHVAT Story

written by
Galia Sabbag

illustrated by
Erin Taylor

To All of You Who
Planted the Shira Seeds.

Text © 2015 by Galia Sabbag
Illustrations © 2015 by Erin Taylor   Visit ErinTaylorIllustrator.com
All rights reserved, including the right of reproduction in whole or in part in any form.

At school, Shira learned about the holiday of Tu Bishvat טוּ בִּשְׁבָט - the fifteenth day of the month of SHVAT שְׁבָט. She learned about trees, plants, flowers, seeds, and taking care of the earth. Her teacher talked about the almond tree שְׁקֵדִיָּה -SHKEDIYA, which is the tree that blooms first in Israel, about the Jewish National Fund (JNF) TZEDAKAH קֶרֶן קַיֶּמֶת לְיִשְׂרָאֵל box, for collecting money to buy trees in Israel, and about the dried fruits we eat on this important holiday.

The class made posters of the seven species שִׁבְעַת הַמִּינִים:

- wheat — חִטָּה
- barley — שְׂעוֹרָה
- DATES — תָּמָר
- olives — זַיִת
- GRAPES — גֶּפֶן
- pomegranites — רִמּוֹן
- figs — תְּאֵנָה

Before they tasted the fruits of trees in Israel, they recited the blessing:

בָּרוּךְ אַתָּה ה' אֱלוֹהֵינוּ מֶלֶךְ הָעוֹלָם בּוֹרֵא פְּרִי הָעֵץ.

However, the most exciting activity was planting trees outside, digging the earth, placing the seedling in the hole, covering it with dirt, watering it, and visiting the growing seedling every day. Shira decided that Tu Bishvat טוּ בִּשְׁבָט is a fantastic holiday!

That afternoon, Shira went with her parents to the supermarket to buy some dried fruits and other groceries. When they were finished, Shira pushed the full cart to the car. She helped put the bags into the trunk and was about to climb into the car.

She looked at the ground right by the car door, and couldn't believe her eyes. A one hundred dollar bill was lying right in front of her!

She picked it up and showed it to her parents. They looked around to see if someone had lost the money.

No one was around.

Her parents told her, "Shira, this money is yours. Use it wisely."

The whole ride home, Shira thought, "What should I do with so much money?"

By the time she arrived home, she had decided exactly what she was going to do with that one hundred dollar bill.

The next morning, in class, Shira asked her teacher for the JNF קֶרֶן קַיֶּמֶת לְיִשְׂרָאֵל TZEDAKAH box. She put the one hundred dollar bill into the box and said happily,

"I would like to donate this money to buy and plant trees in Israel, our homeland!"

Her teacher was impressed, and her classmates cheered in admiration. When the principal heard about Shira's donation, he was amazed.

Most children would rather have bought a toy or candy, but not Shira!

Shira had done a MITZVAH מִצְוָה - a big one.

The principal called the JNF קֶרֶן קַיֶּמֶת לְיִשְׂרָאֵל office. He told them the story about Shira, and they made arrangements for a rally in her honor.

A few days later, on Tu Bishvat טוּ בִּשְׁבָט the entire school was in the gym, with television cameras from the local news, newspaper reporters, and the JNF קֶרֶן קַיֶּמֶת לְיִשְׂרָאֵל representatives.

The JNF קֶרֶן קַיֶּמֶת לְיִשְׂרָאֵל representatives called Shira to the stage, and told her she had done an extraordinary MITZVAH מִצְוָה. They gave her a special certificate, shook her hand, and took lots of photos.

She appeared on television that night. Soon after, her story was in the newspaper. Shira was extremely happy and proud and so were her parents.

A few years later, when Shira visited Israel for her Bat Mitzvah celebration, she went to visit all of her trees - all the trees her big mitzvah מִצְוָה had helped to plant.

The story behind the story:

The author, Galia Sabbag, is a veteran Hebrew teacher of over fifteen years at The Davis Academy, a Reform Jewish Day School in Atlanta, GA. During her years of teaching, she has come across some beautiful, thought-provoking examples of how school affects families and their home life and how children grow in Jewish knowledge and spirituality. By witnessing these "aha" moments and/or by listening to parents' and grandparents' anecdotes, a series of stories emerged, and became lovable "Shira." She is the culmination of all Mrs. Sabbag's students throughout the years. Most of the stories in the series are real ones that actually happened to real students, interwoven with the author's creativity.

Shira opens young readers' minds to the incredible gift of giving. Shira gives wholeheartedly, not expecting to receive anything in return. It is wonderful to see such kindness in such a young child. Before deciding what to do, Shira thinks it through. She asks herself what would be best. Shira's thought before action is also a powerful message for our young children. This really lovely story takes place during the beautiful festival of Tu B'shvat.

Mrs. Sabbag's stories are imbued with and enriched by Hebrew words, songs, greetings, and blessings. These stories will appeal to children in Jewish preschools, Sunday school or Jewish day schools and of course, in every Jewish home.

If you enjoyed *Shira and the Trees* you will love other stories in the Shira series: *Miracle for Shira* and *RIMON for Shira*. The eBooks are available on Amazon Kindle and on Barnes and Noble Nook. Printed copies are available through the website.

Please check out the website:
www.shirasseries.com
twitter: @shirasSeries
or the Facebook page: www.facebook.com/Shira.series

Made in the USA
Middletown, DE
06 January 2019